RUBANK EDUCATIONAL LIBRARY No. 140

SELECTED STUDIES

Advanced Etudes, Scales and Arpeggios in All Major and All Minor Keys

FLUTE

by H. Voxman

ADVANCED ETUDES

SPECIAL STUDIES

SCALES AND ARPEGGIOS

HAL•LEONARD® CORPORATION
7777 W. BLUEMOUND RD. P.O. BOX 13819 MILWAUKEE, WI 53213

SELECTED STUDIES FOR FLUTE

C MAJOR

Heinze

Köhler

* Gradually accelerate until the fifth measure (main tempo).

A MINOR

SARABANDE

(Sonata for Flute)

Bach

BOURRÉE ANGLAISE
(Sonata for Flute)

Bach

G MAJOR

Valse lento
Köhler
con eleganza
1
Fine
(second time)
Fine
mf
tr
tr
tr
tr
f
f
allarg.
D. S. al Fine
rit.

Allegretto mosso
Köhler
p
p
allarg. presto
Tempo di Valse
Tempo I
rall.
p
f
p
p
f
p
rit
Piú vivo
mf
f
p

E MINOR

Largo lagrimoso

Ferling

Allegretto
Köhler
mf marcando sempre la prima della note legate
(piu animato on D.C.)
CODA
D.C. al Coda
rall.
f
incalzando
sempre fino al fine
f

F MAJOR

Lento e cantabile

Köhler

Allegro
Bach-Schindler
f molto leggiero
dim.
p
simile
cresc
mf
f
dim
p
mf
p
mf
p
p
mf
p
cresc
mf
mf
f
f
ff
poco riten.
p

D MINOR

Lento (♩= 54)
Andersen
p espress.
p
espress.
mf
p
mf
f
p
mf
lunga
tr
p
tranquillo
morendo
pp

Karg-Elert

Un poco mosso, ma non brillante
mf
f
f
cresc
rfz
p amabile
f
f
f
p
f
p
f
p
rall.

D MAJOR

Allegro non troppo (♩= 132)

Bach-Schindler

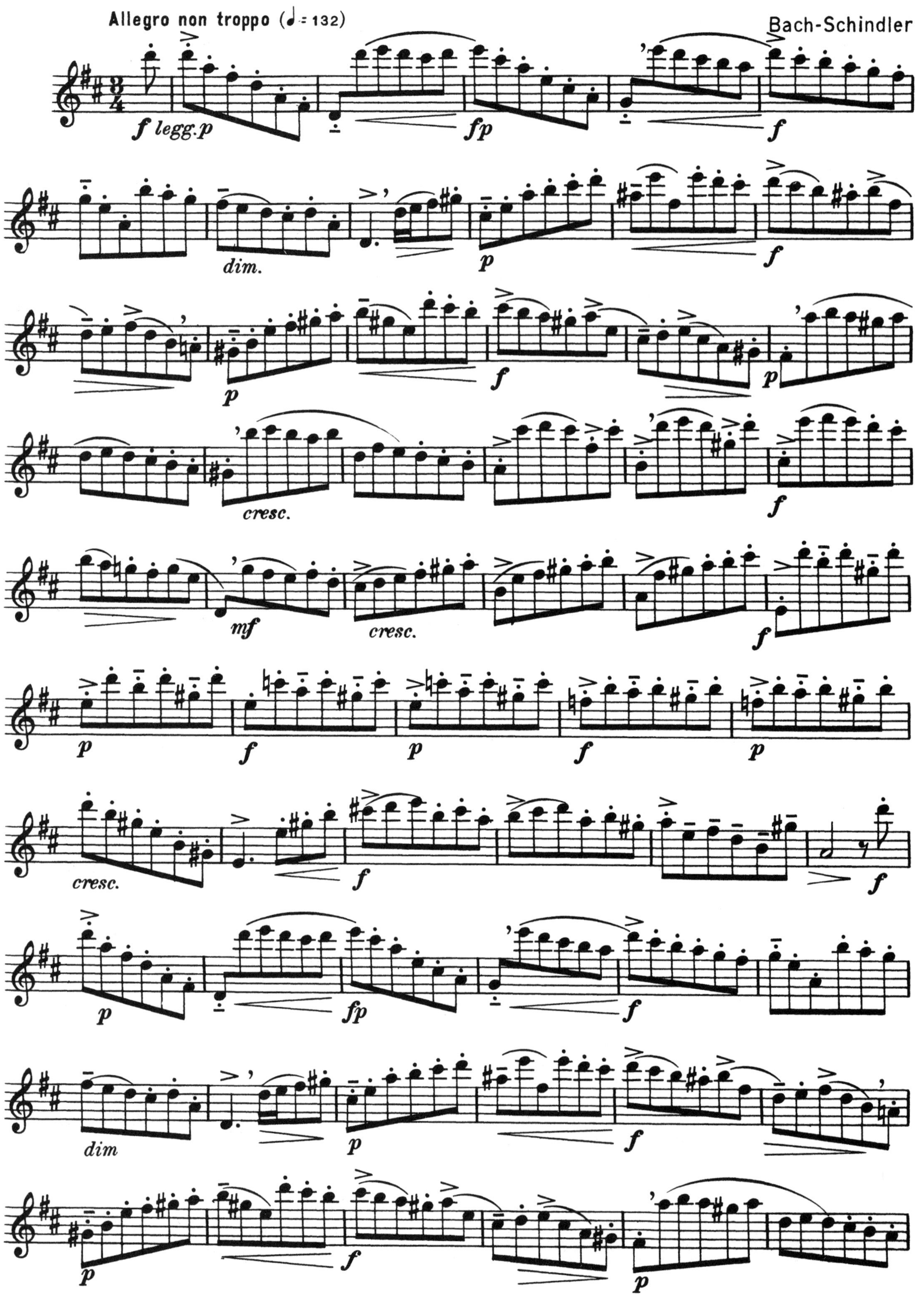

cresc.
f
mf
cresc.
f
p
f
p
f
p
cresc.
f
f
p
cresc.
f
dim
p
cresc.
f
f
dim.
p
mf
fz
dim
pp
cresc. sempre
f
p
f
p
f
p
cresc.
f
IIda volta riten.

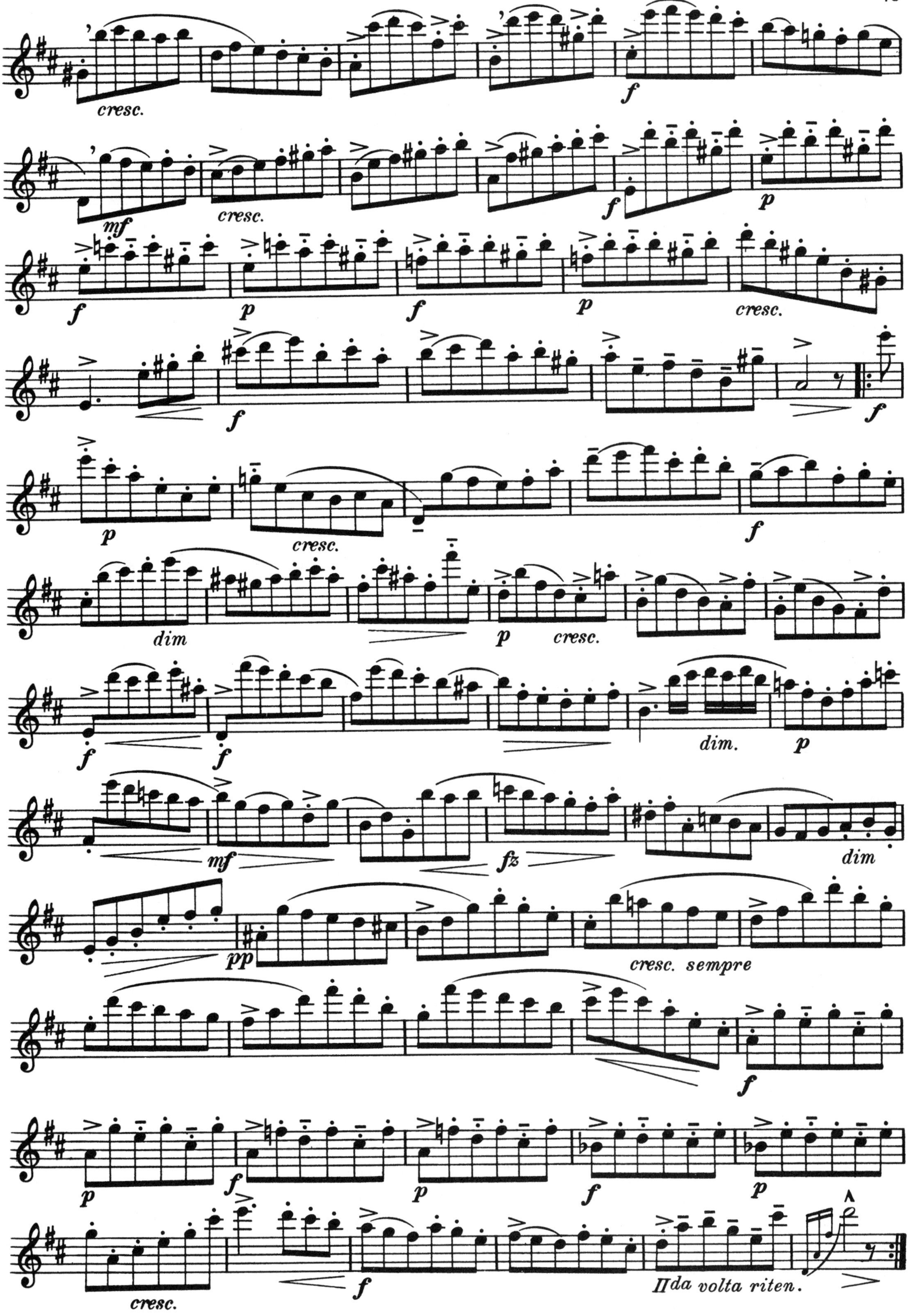

Moderato
Köhler
f capriccioso
rall.
D.C. al Coda

Andersen

Adagio (♩ = 46)

Gariboldi
Allegro vivo
p
f
ff
p
dim.
p
f
p
cresc.
p
rit.
Poco meno mosso
con anima
cresc.

rall.
Tempo I
p
f
ff
p
dim.
p
p
f
p e cresc. sempre
tr
f

B♭ MAJOR

Köhler

GIGA

Bach

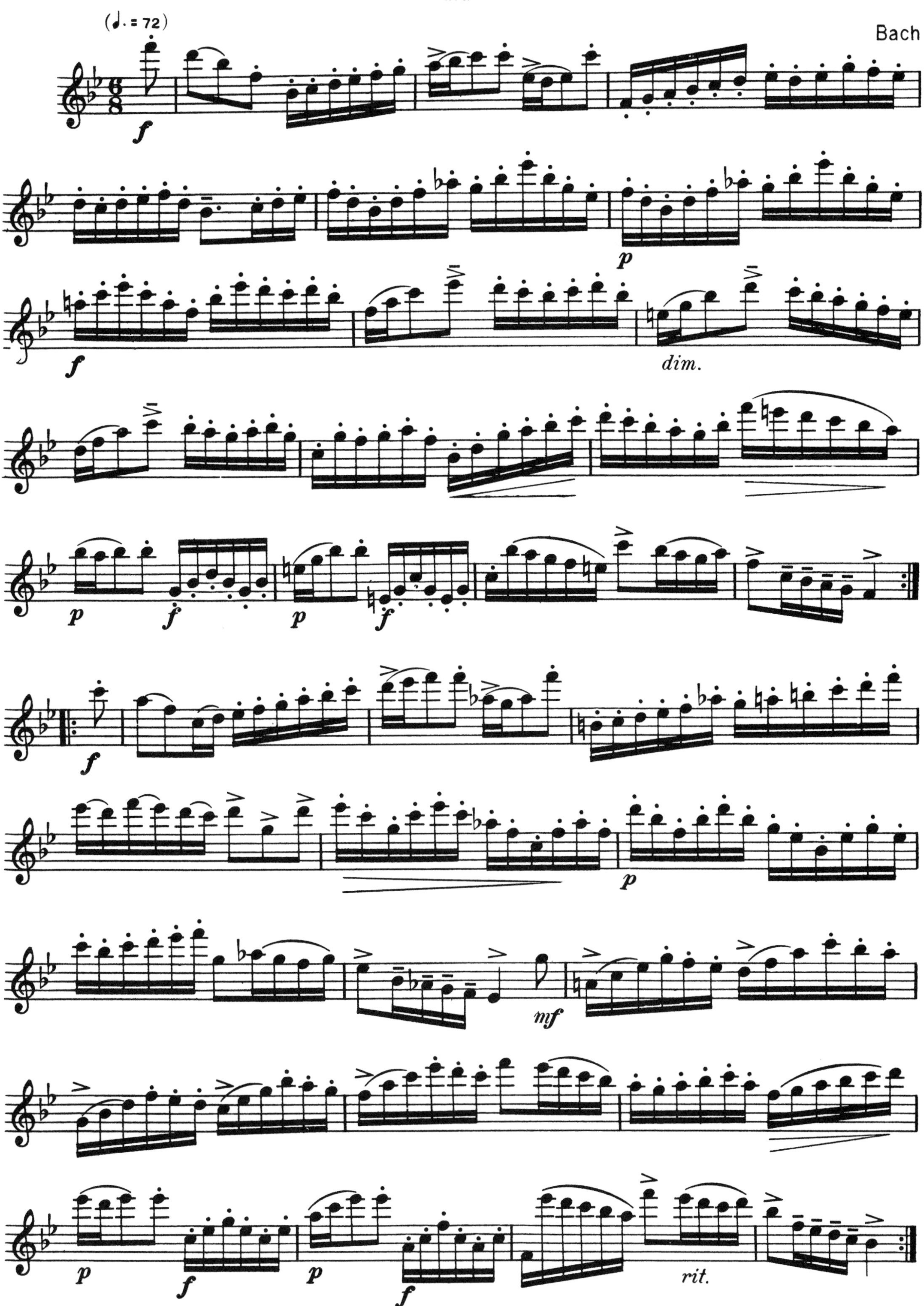

G MINOR

Moderato assai (♩ = 96)
Andersen
f risoluto
f
f
ff
f
f
ff
ff
ff
1
2
f
f
f
ff
f
ff
ff

Köhler

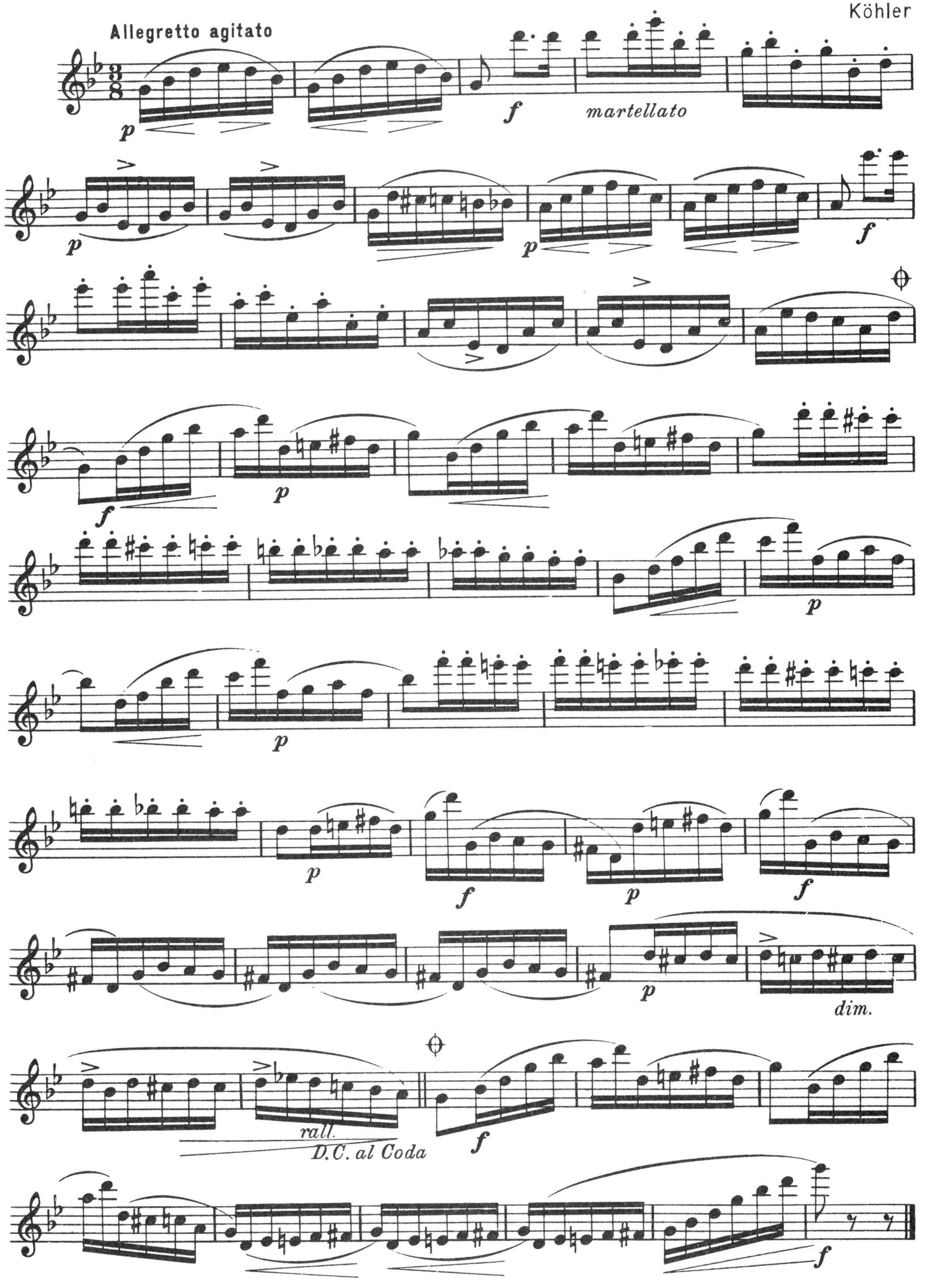
Allegretto agitato
p
f
martellato
p
p
f
f
p
p
p
p
f
p
f
p
dim.
rall.
D.C. al Coda
f
f

A MAJOR

Köhler

Largo
Leggiero e veloce
Karg-Elert
pp
mp
mf
f
pp
f
p
pp

F♯ MINOR

Köhler

Vivace
Kummer
p
sf
sf
sf
sf
sf
sf
p
cres - cen - do
fz
fz
cres - cen -
do
fz
fz
fz
fz
fz
fz
ff
p
dolce
tr
tr
tr
p
sf
sf
p
f
ff

E♭ MAJOR

GIGUE

p
p
cresc.
f
p
cresc. sempre
f
p
largamente
a tempo
f
ff
legg.
p
f
p
p
dim.
pp
p
cresc.
f
ff
IIda volta riten.

Prill
Allegretto
p
pp
f
mf
f
ff

C MINOR
Drouet
Adagio cantabile
p
con espressione

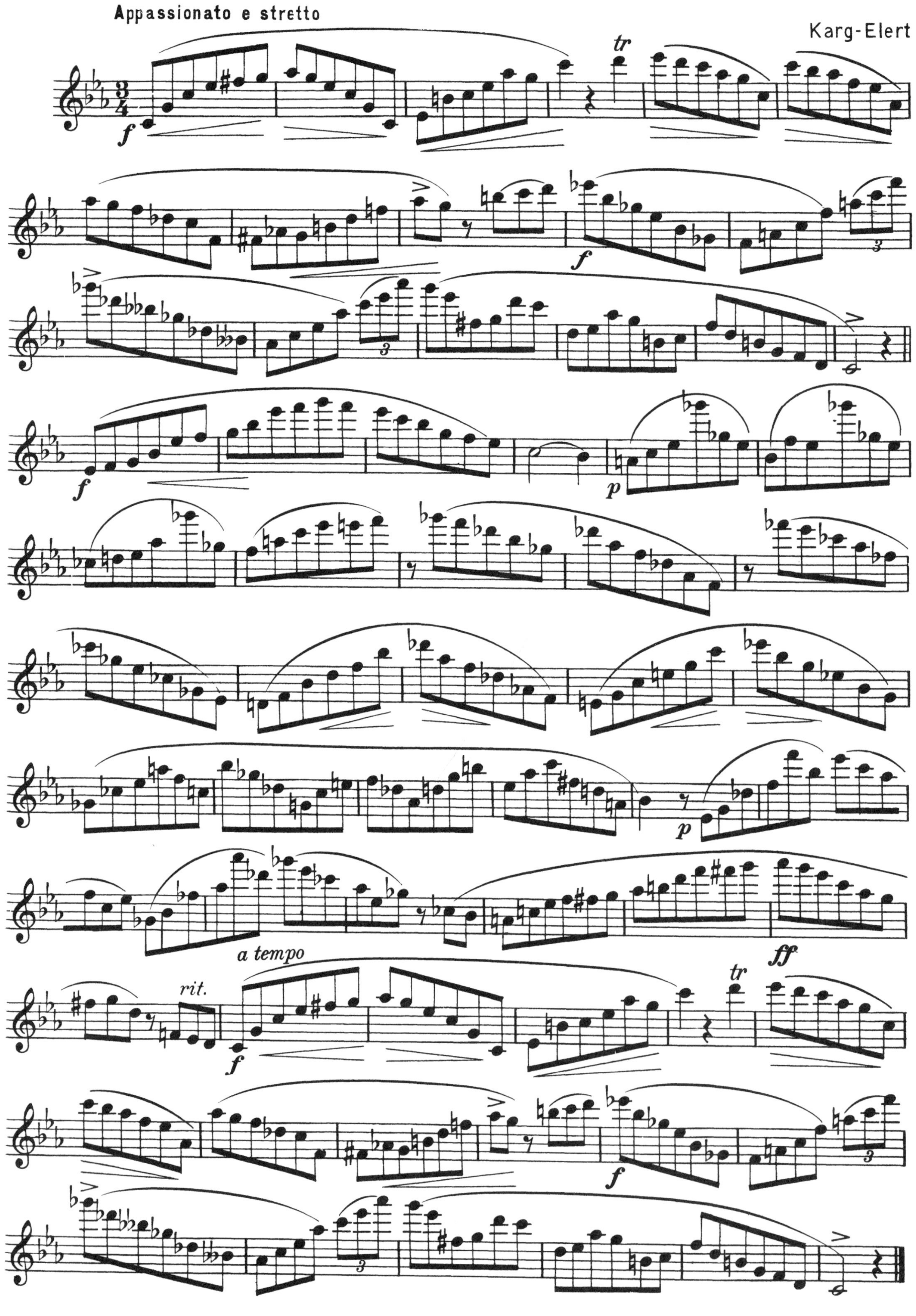
Appassionato e stretto
Karg-Elert
f
tr
f
f
p
p
p
ff
rit.
a tempo
f
tr
f

E MAJOR

RUSSIAN DANCE

Köhler

Drouet
Allegro
f
simile

C♯ MINOR

Andersen

ROMANZA

Andersen

dim.
pp
tranquillo
pp
a tempo
mf
p dolce
p
cresc.
p
lamentabile
cresc.
f
pp
dim.
p dolce
cresc.
dim.
p
p
p
mf
dim.
pp

A♭ MAJOR

Andante cantabile (𝅗𝅥 = 69)

Soussmann

Allegretto
Andersen
Fine
D. C. al Fine

F MINOR

GIGUE

Allegro (♩.= 69)

Bach

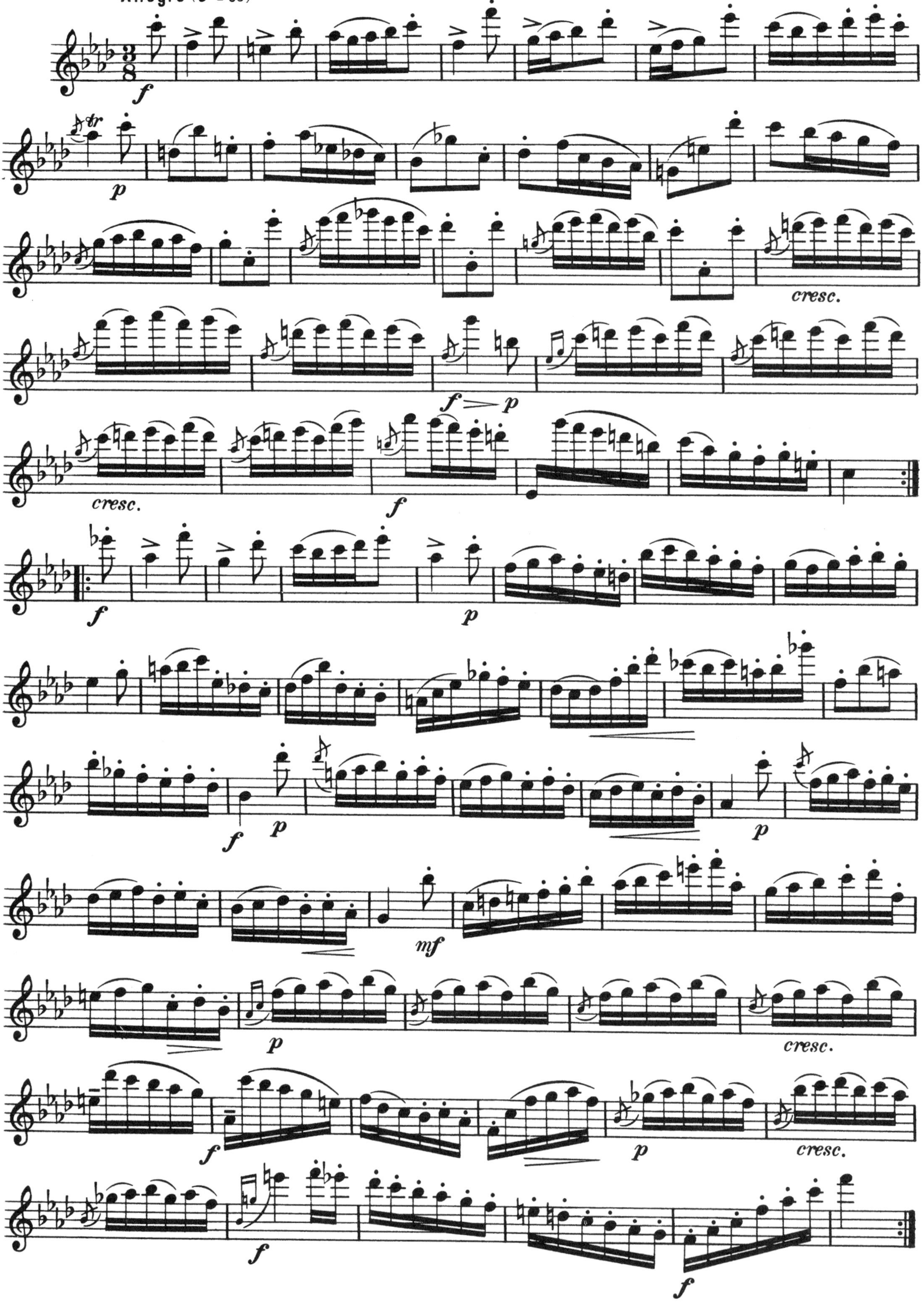

f *p* *cresc.* *f* *p* *cresc.* *f* *f* *p* *f* *p* *p* *mf* *p* *cresc.* *f* *p* *cresc.* *f* *f*

Allegro
Andersen
f
p
f
p
f
p
f
p
f
f
Fine
f
p
f
p
f
f
f
f
f
p
f
p
f
f
f
f
f
D.C. al Fine

B MAJOR

In tempo di Walzer
Karg-Elert
p
grazioso
p
morbido
f
p
f
scherzoso
p

Allegro
Drouet
simile
f
p
dim.

G# MINOR

Presto molto (♩. = 138)
Andersen
f adirato (angrily)
p
f
p
f
p
f
p
f
p
cresc
f
1
Fine
Fine
ff

mf
cresc.
ff
mf
cresc
f
p
f
p
f
p
f
p
f
p
f
p
f
dim
p
f
dim
p
f
dim
p
f
D. C. al Fine

Moderato (𝅗𝅥. = 58)
Bach
p
più f
cresc.
f
dim.
mf
p
cres - cen - do
f
p
più f
cresc
f
dim.
mf
p
cres - cen - do
f
mf
mf
dim.
p
p
cresc.
f

D♭ MAJOR

Allegro (𝅗𝅥. = 60)

Bach

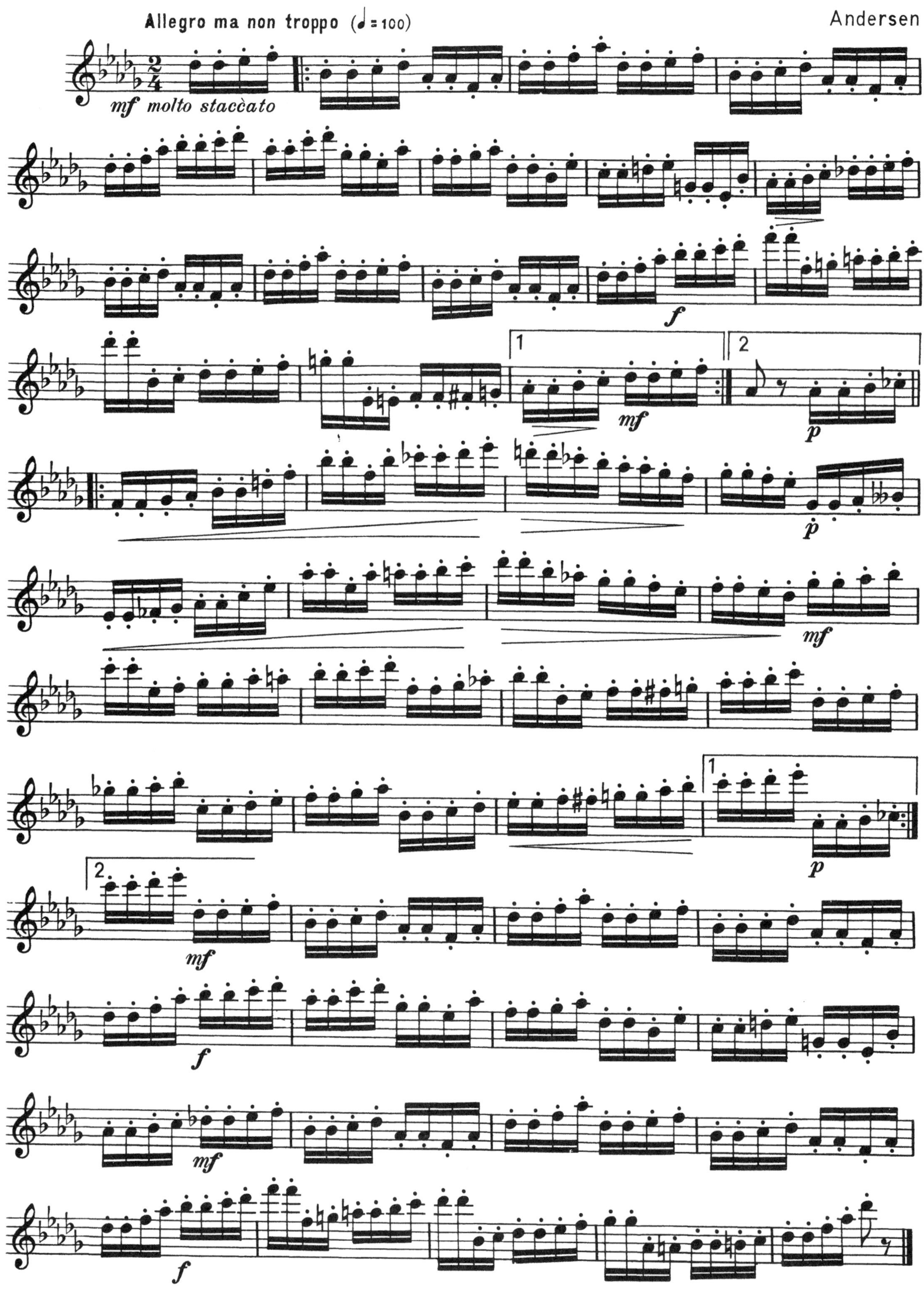
Allegro ma non troppo (♩= 100)
Andersen
mf molto staccato
mf
p
f
mf
p
p
mf
p
mf
f
mf
f
1
2
1
2

B♭ MINOR

Heinze

Allegro
Heinze
mf stacc.
f
cresc.
ff
1
f
ff
marc.
mf
fz

F♯ MAJOR

Ferling

Velocissimo e frizzante (sharply)
Karg-Elert
pp
f
pp
sfz

D♯ MINOR

Drouet

SCHERZO

Heinze

G♭ MAJOR

Heinze

Heinze

E♭ MINOR

Köhler

Allegretto vivo

p ff p ff

con elegonza

rit.

a tempo

a tempo

rit.

p dim. D. C. al 𝄌 p f

p

dim.

Prill
Allegretto
tr
p
6

tr
tr
tr
tr
tr
tr
tr
tr
tr
tr
tr
tr
tr
tr
tr
tr
tr
tr

DOUBLE TONGUING

Köhler

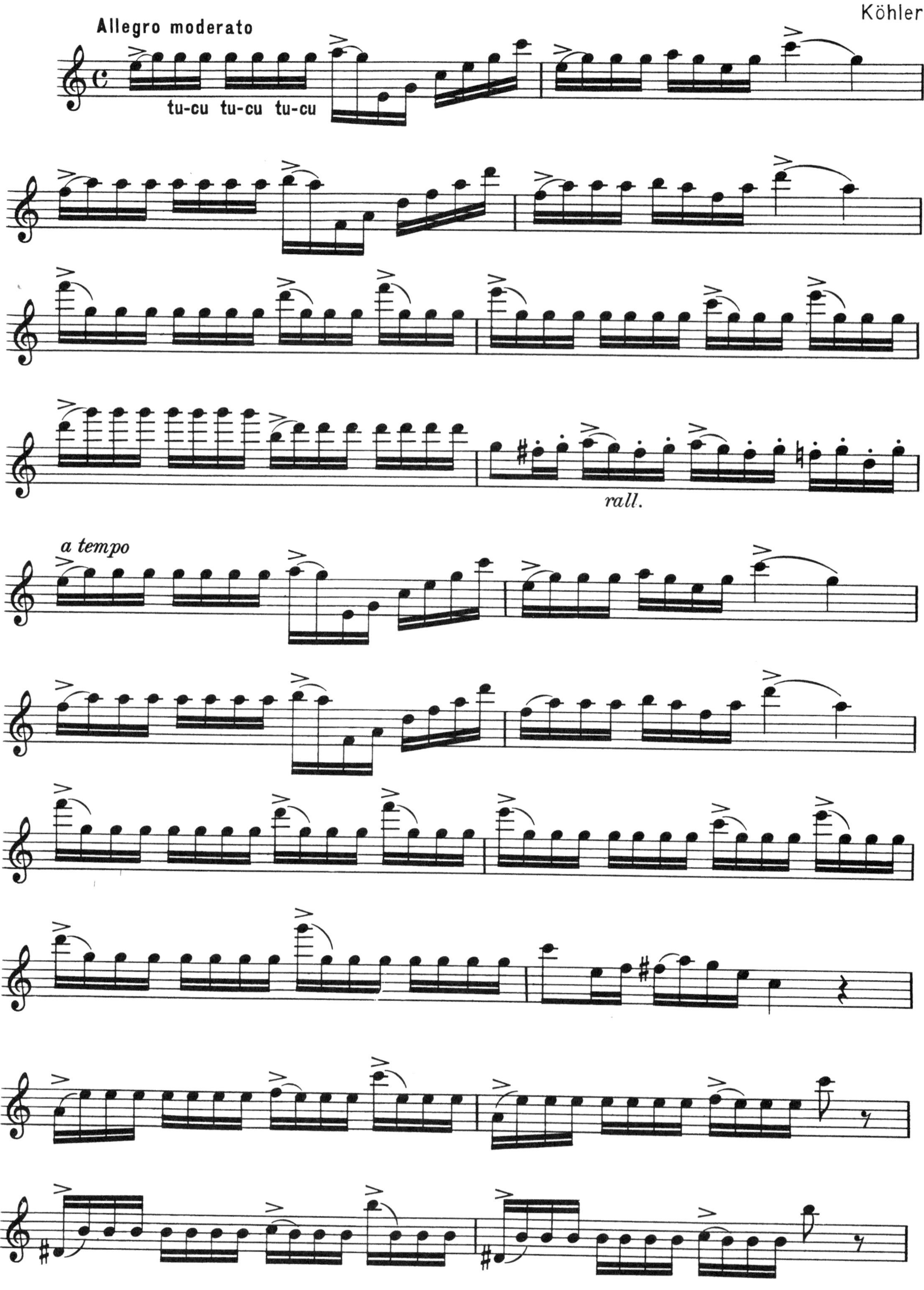

dim.
a tempo

THE WIND

a tempo
rall.

CAPRICCIO IN D MAJOR

Allegro giusto

Karg-Elert

SCALES

The use of a metronome with the following exercises is highly recommended.

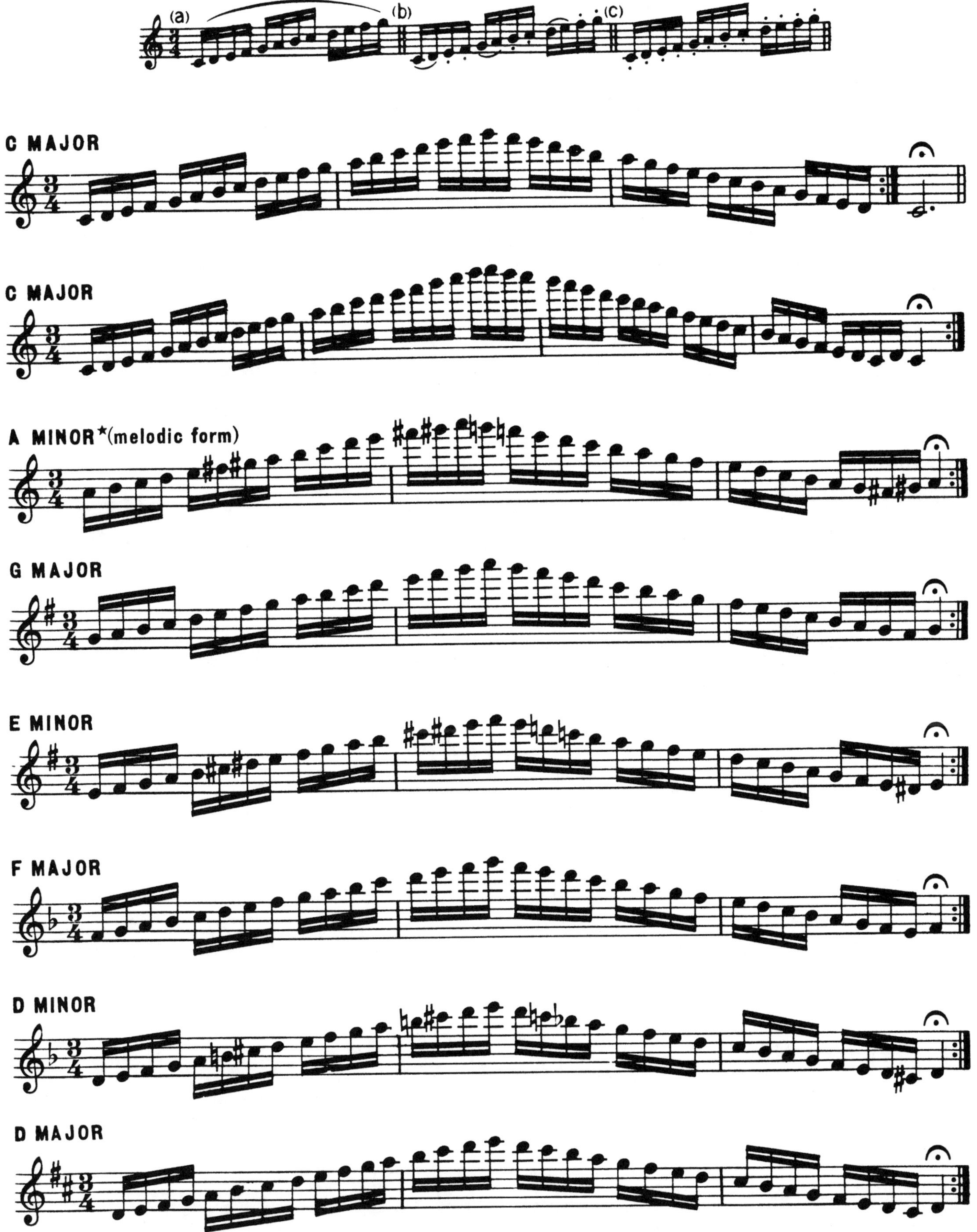

* All minor scale exercises should also be practiced in the harmonic form.

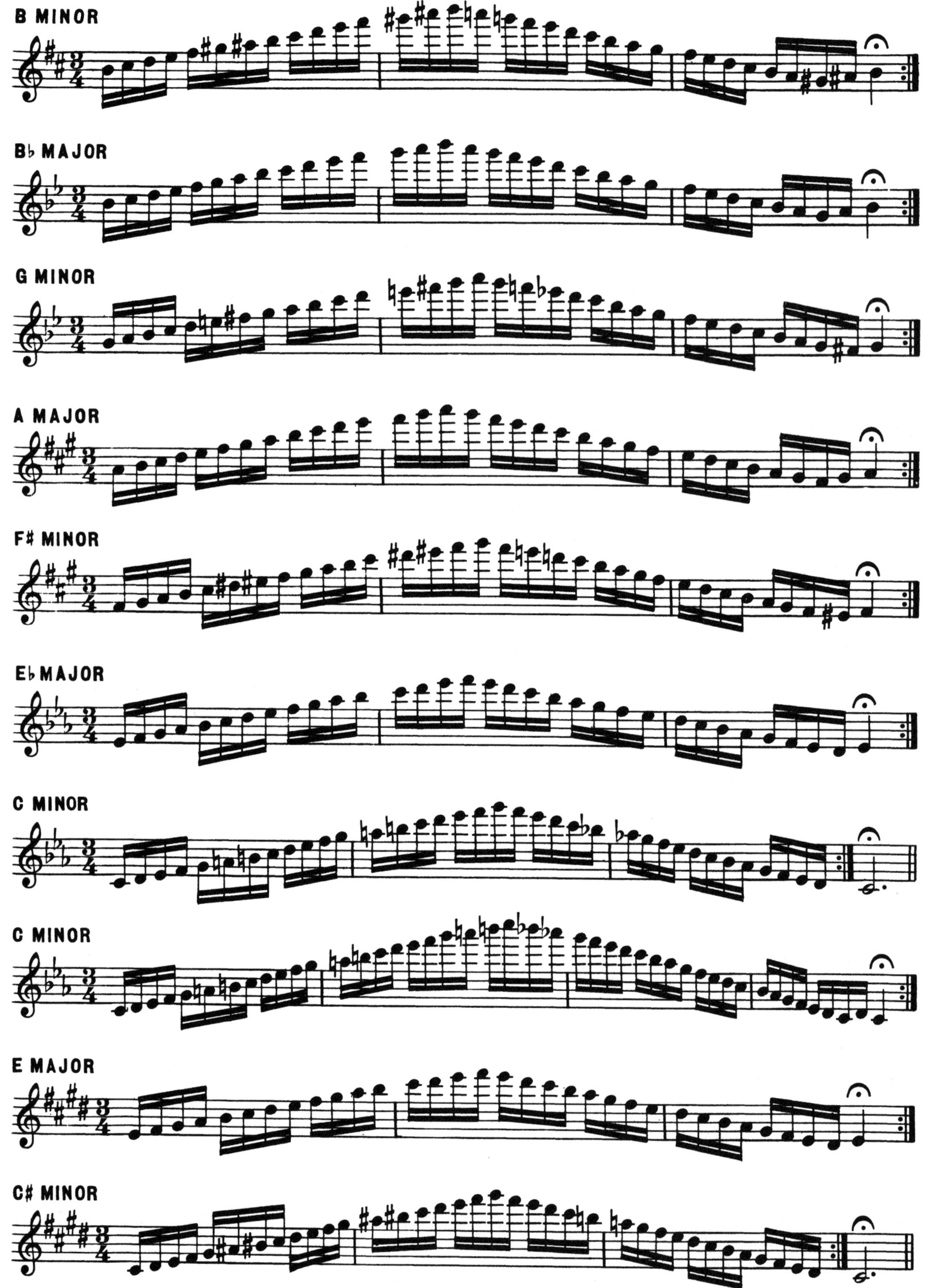
B MINOR
B♭ MAJOR
G MINOR
A MAJOR
F♯ MINOR
E♭ MAJOR
C MINOR
C MINOR
E MAJOR
C♯ MINOR

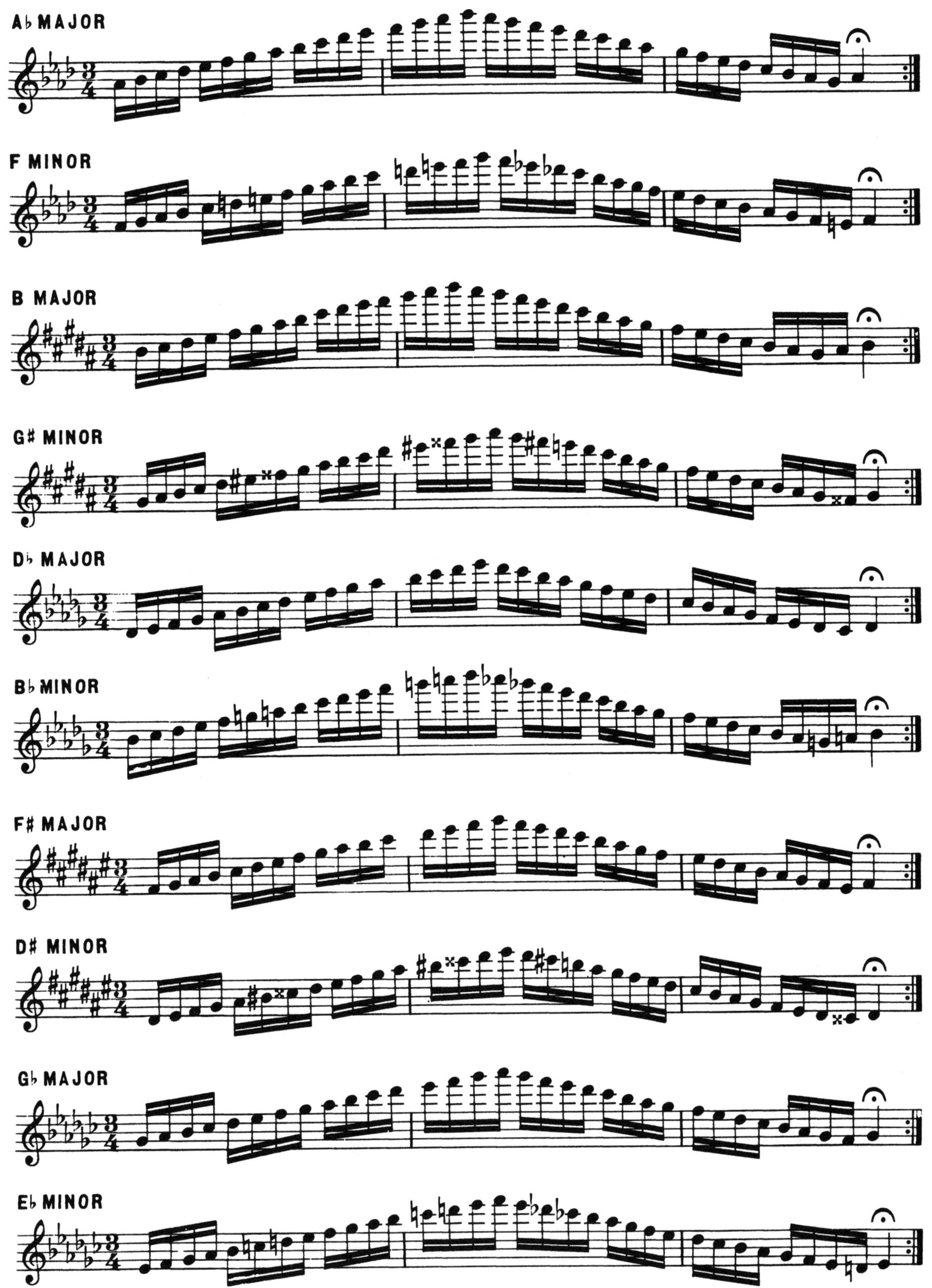
A♭ MAJOR
F MINOR
B MAJOR
G♯ MINOR
D♭ MAJOR
B♭ MINOR
F♯ MAJOR
D♯ MINOR
G♭ MAJOR
E♭ MINOR

SCALES IN THIRDS

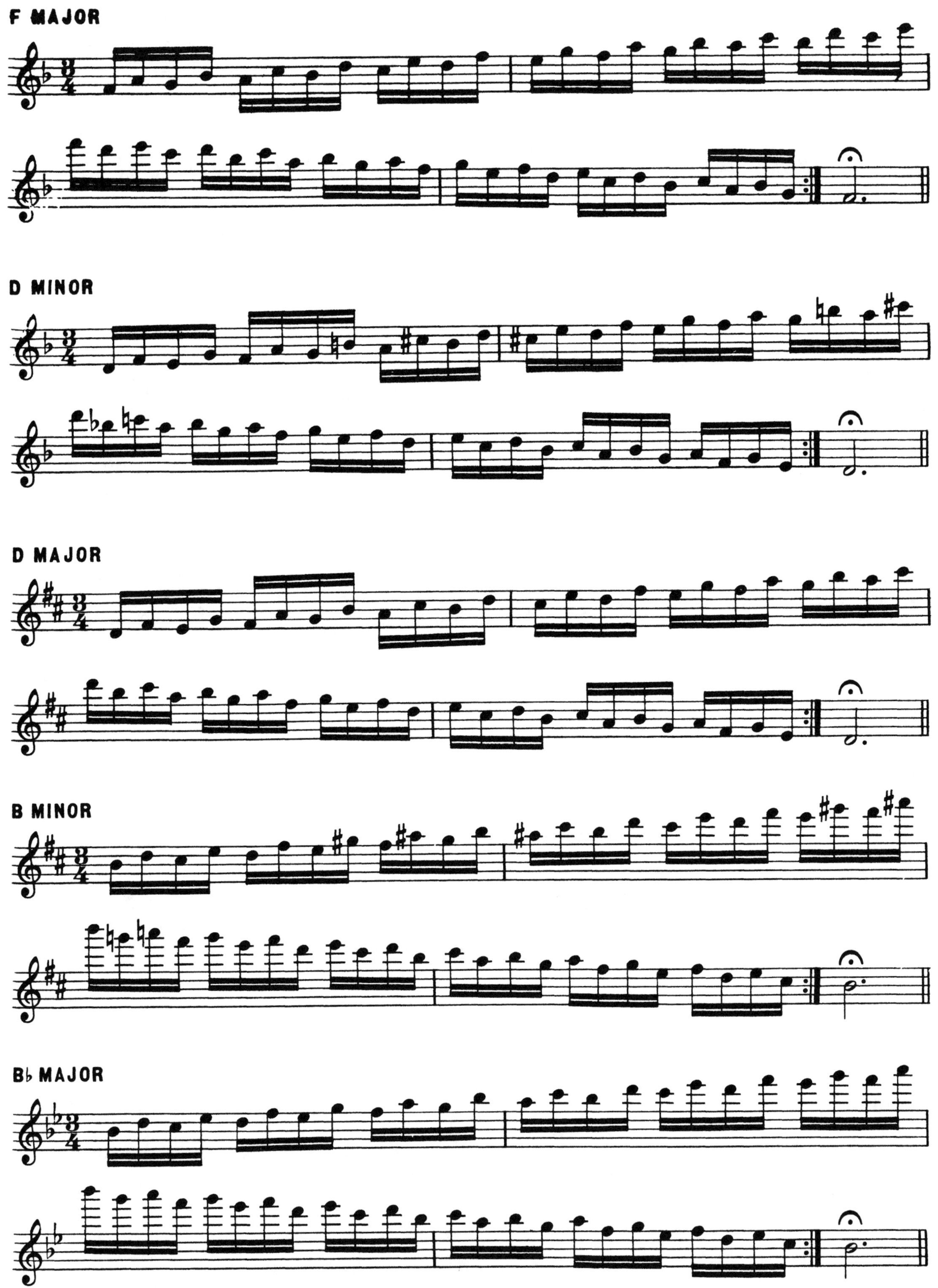
F MAJOR
D MINOR
D MAJOR
B MINOR
B♭ MAJOR

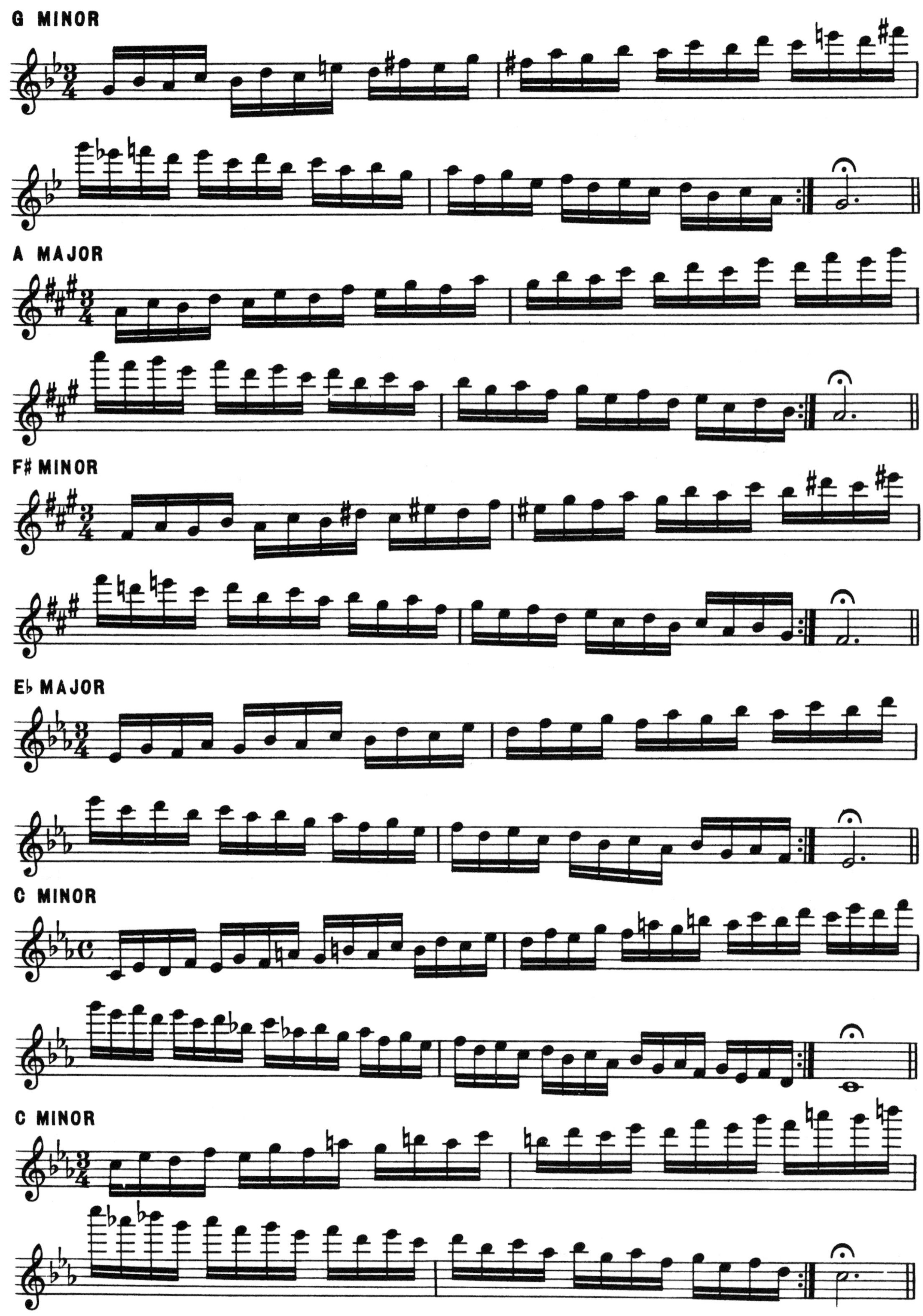
G MINOR
A MAJOR
F# MINOR
E♭ MAJOR
C MINOR
C MINOR

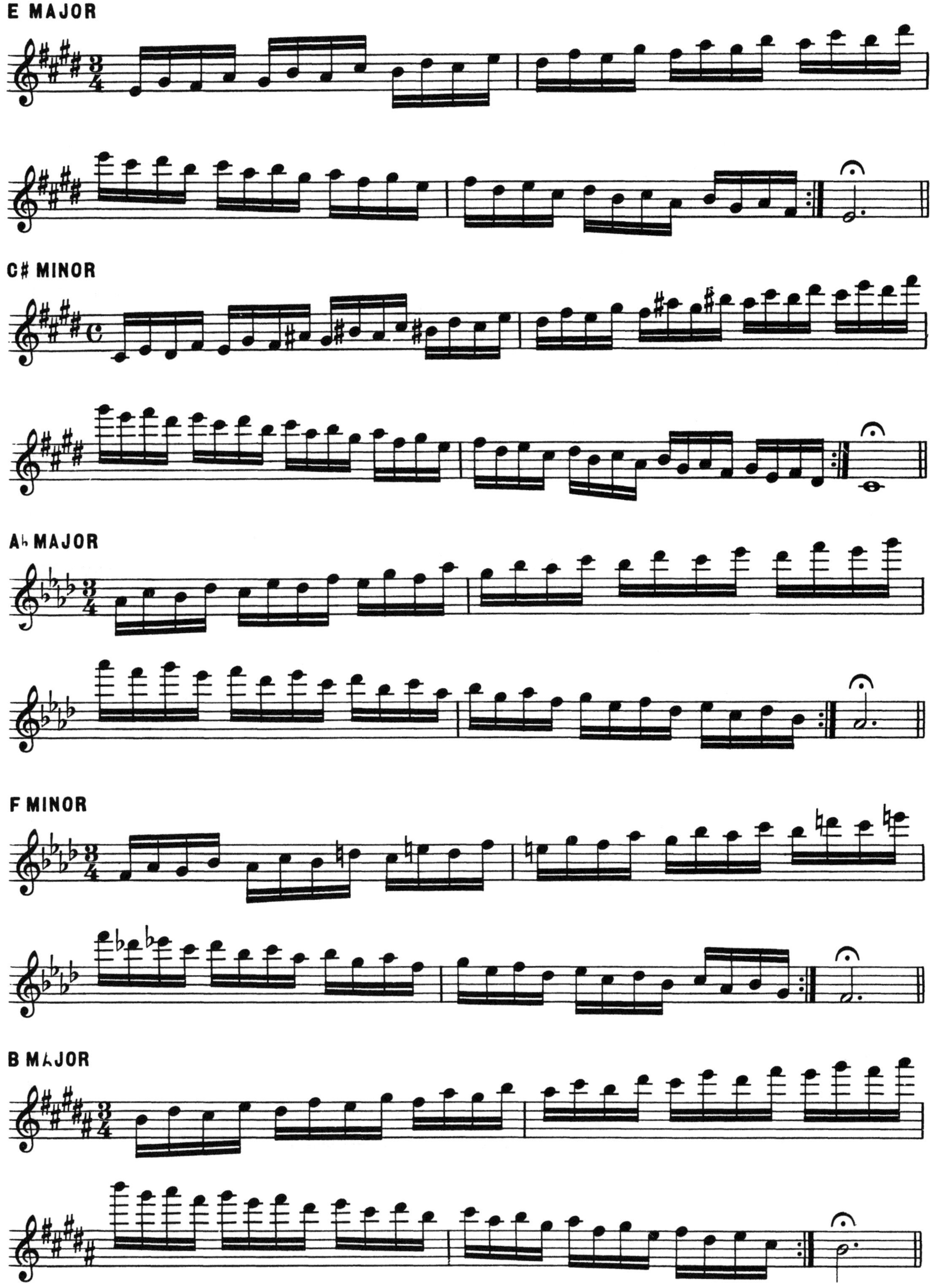
E MAJOR
C# MINOR
A♭ MAJOR
F MINOR
B MAJOR

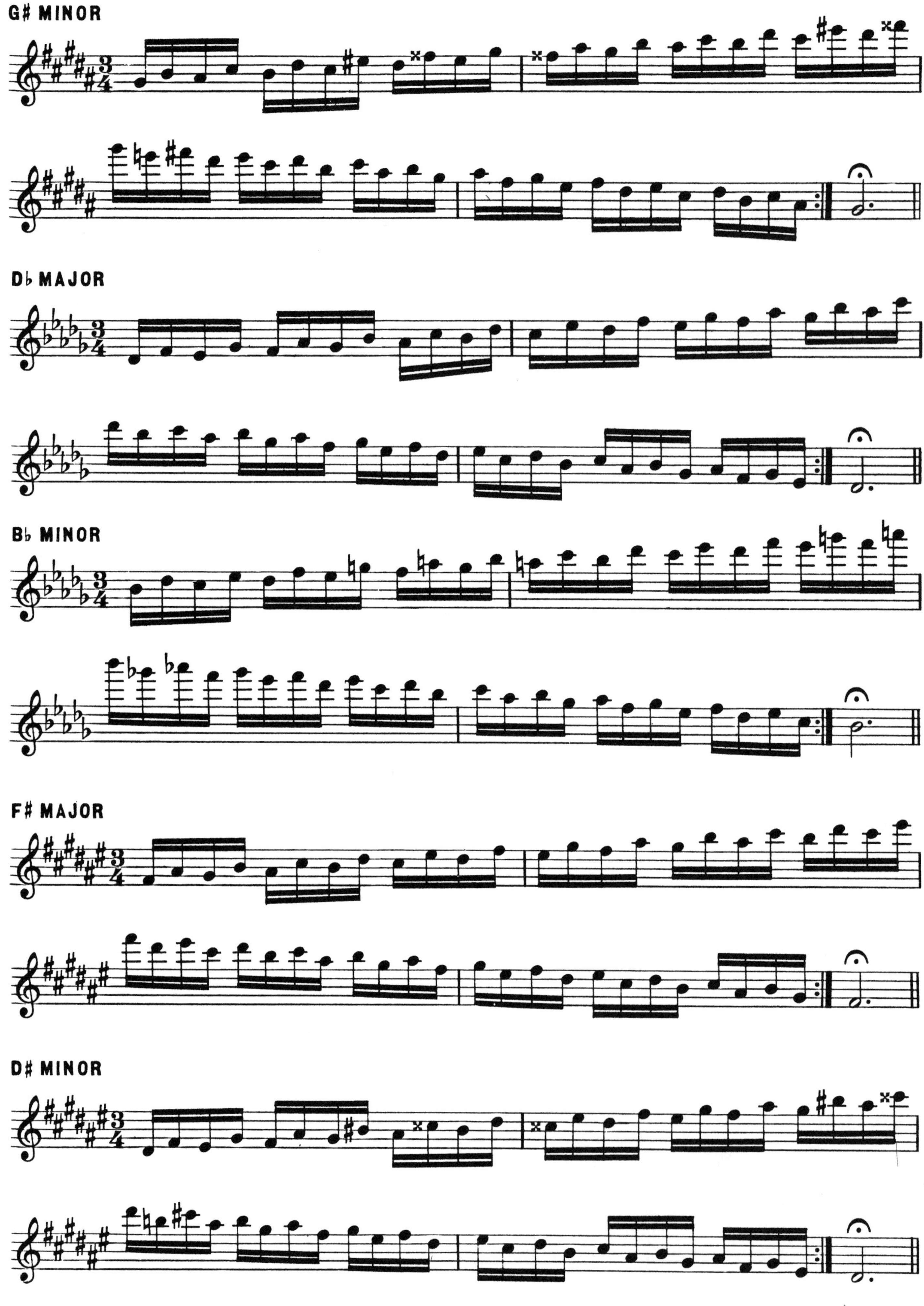
G# MINOR
D♭ MAJOR
B♭ MINOR
F# MAJOR
D# MINOR

G♭ MAJOR
E♭ MINOR
MAJOR THIRDS
MINOR THIRDS
Intervals derived from whole-tone scale.

ARPEGGIOS

(a)
(b)
(c)
C MAJOR
C MAJOR
A MINOR
G MAJOR
E MINOR
F MAJOR
D MINOR
D MAJOR
B MINOR

B♭ MAJOR
G MINOR
A MAJOR
F♯ MINOR
E♭ MAJOR
C MINOR
C MINOR
E MAJOR
C♯ MINOR
A♭ MAJOR
F MINOR

B MAJOR
G# MINOR
D♭ MAJOR
B♭ MINOR
F# MAJOR
D# MINOR
G♭ MAJOR
E♭ MINOR
Arpeggio of the Augmented 5th on C.
Arpeggio of the Augmented 5th on D♭.